John 3:16

For GOD so loved the world that he gave his one and only son, that whoever believes in him shall not perish but have eternal life.

To GOD be the glory!

This book is dedicated to all the fur babies, and those that love and care for them

This book belongs to:

_____ ● _____

The Adventures of Mr. Wilson

A Children's Series
Series 1

By Dennis and Dolores Horine
Illustrated by Gwendolyne (Wendy) Dean

Hello!

My name is Mr. Wilson. I am a Himalayan cat,
a very special breed with many special needs.

This is my Story.

Life has been so easy for me.
I have been an "indoors only" cat
all my life.
All I've had to do is lay around and let
my humans care for me.

Not long ago
My life was turned
upside down.

My humans moved
away, leaving me here
by myself.

Next thing I knew,

my house was being invaded!

Now I am in charge

of these two humans

and these four

annoying cats.

Good grief!

This is when my adventures began.

Let me tell you about my day!
It all started early this morning when my two humans decided to wake up and turn on all the lights, super early!

So, I got up and stretched really well.

The two sister cats growled loudly! Why are they so grouchy?

I made my way to the food room
my humans call the Kitchen.
This is where all the delicious food
is served to me

And everyone else too, I guess.
Salmon for breakfast this morning!

MY FAVORITE!

They are SO annoying!
Especially this old man cat they call
"Treecat"
What kind of a name is Treecat?
Did they find him in a tree?

He eats ALL the food,
Then the girl cats start meowing
to the humans for more!

I have these furry little
creatures digging holes
in my backyard.

My humans do not like them,
so when I see them
I chase them!

They run under the fence
into my neighbors' yard.

When it's sunny outside
I like to take my first nap
under this table.
It has a glass top and is so warm.

Oh my bananas! Someone left the side door cracked open.

I will just give it a push and go explore the neighborhood!

My family finally let me in!
Now for a snack and...
another nap.

What a day it has been!
Tomorrow will hold new adventures.
Until then, goodnight, friends!

Treecat Publishing LLC
www.treecatpublishing.com

The Adventures of Mr. Wilson

Text Copyright 2018 Dennis and Dolores Horine
Illustration Copyright 2018 Gwendolyne (Wendy) Dean

All rights reserved

No parts of this publication may be reproduced, stored in a retrieval system, or transmitted in any form or by any means, electronic, mechanical, photocopying, recording, or otherwise, without the prior written permission of the copyright owner.

This book is sold subject to the condition that it shall not, by way of trade or otherwise, be lent, resold, hired out, or otherwise circulated without the publisher's prior consent in any form of binding or cover other than that in which it is published and without a similar condition including this condition being imposed on the subsequent purchaser. Under no circumstances may any part of this book be photocopied for resale.

www.ingramcontent.com/pod-product-compliance
Lightning Source LLC
LaVergne TN
LVHW072104070426
835508LV00003B/267